The FEMALE Fool

10 Reasons Why You Aren't Attracting A Good Christian Man

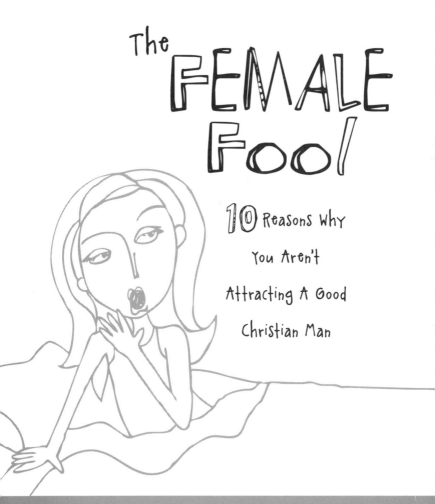

The FEMALE Fool

10 Reasons Why You Aren't Attracting A Good Christian Man

Melissa Diane Hudson

CREATION HOUSE

(August 19 2012)

THE FEMALE FOOL by Melissa Diane Hudson
Published by Creation House Books
A Charisma Media Company
600 Rinehart Road
Lake Mary, Florida 32746
www.charismamedia.com

Scripture quotations are from the King James Version of the Bible.

Design Director: Bill Johnson
Cover design by Nancy Panaccione

Visit the author by e-mail: christianwriter33@yahoo.com

Library of Congress Cataloging-in-Publication Data:
2011923396
International Standard Book Number: 978-1-61638-482-1

11 12 13 14 15 — 9 8 7 6 5 4 3 2
Printed in Canada

TABLE OF CONTENTS

DEDICATION

In memory of my loving husband

Dr. Curtis Hudson Jr.

December 26, 1970–December 31, 2010

You are truly missed, but never forgotten. I will always love you.

ACKNOWLEDGMENTS

FIRST AND FOREMOST, I want to express my unceasing love to God, who is the greatest blessing in my life and who made it possible for me to create this work so that it can truly make a difference to so many females. The reason this book was written is to explain to females how to attract a good Christian man led by God.

When I met my husband, I was not out in the world searching or looking for a man. God knew what kind of man I desired and when the time was right, we crossed one another's path. We later married after two years of friendship, two years of dating, and two years of engagement. No divorce or legal separation split us apart. I loved him unconditionally and honored my marriage vows through faithfulness, sickness and in health until death did us apart. God blessed our six years of marriage and to this union a son was born. It is not hard to attract a Christian man, but you must put God first and allow Him to send you that man.

I also would like to thank my late loving husband, who I will forever love truly, Dr. Curtis Hudson Jr. for presenting his helpful input and views on this subject matter from a man's perspective. Without his overall feedback, I would never have known to think outside the box in certain areas. My son, Curtis Hudson III, one of the greatest blessings in our life who I love dearly, is such a wonderful special baby who allowed me the time many mornings and evenings to craft this material into what God required.

My siblings, Calvin Dennis and Captain Jennifer Dennis, thank you all for your kind support: I am always grateful.

To all the people who will purchase a copy of this book, I truly thank you in advance and hope that you receive a thoughtful message that will impact and empower you life forever. Be blessed!

INTRODUCTION
The Female Fool

MY PURPOSE FOR writing this book is to educate females on how to walk in elegance, grace and modesty just like Godly women if they would like to one day attract a good Christian man. Men have been prowling for women since biblical times, and as every year passes, the hunt to gain their attention grows stronger. Yet, legion of females feel as though they have to engage in sexual activity with men in order to keep them. But what females fail to realize is that there are godly standards that are so important when choosing a life partner.

First of all, there is a tremendous difference in character between a female and a woman when it comes to a Christian man deciphering between the two when choosing a future mate. In this book, *The Female Fool*, I explain ten reasons why *women* always attract the good men, whereas *females* attract the duds. Indeed, following and obeying the biblical principles of God allows good relationships to manifest into wonderful marriages. The foundation for a good marriage begins when the two begin dating. How one dates sometimes determines what kind of marriage one will have.

Females are accustomed to saying, "There are no good men in the world," or "All the good men are taken." That statement is simply untrue. The world has available good Christian men who are searching for good Christian women, not females. Having a close-knit relationship with God allows one to develop an eye of discernment that will differentiate what is real and unreal. The devil comes in all types of forms to manipulate the mind so that he can get into the spirit. Females cannot continue to live by the world's standards and expect to receive greatness and favor from God. What makes a woman a woman is not the number of men she has slept with or the number of children she has birthed, but it is that virtuous glow that shines brightly upon her face, manifesting into her soul that only God can create.

Reason 1

YOU'RE THE HUNTER LOOKING FOR PREY

I T HAS BEEN said time and time again that there are no good men available who are willing to treat women like precious gold. The wrong men seem to appear out of nowhere on some females' doorsteps, carrying more than a lifetime of baggage and heartache. Females meet Mr. Wrong a lot because they overlook Mr. Might Be, Mr. Maybe, or Mr. Right. First of all, there is a huge difference between a woman and a female when it comes to her moral values and Godly principles.

To begin, a female has the genetic makeup of a specific species, relating to the sex that bears the young. There are distinctive types of females such as: a heifer, which is a female cow; a hen is a female chicken; a bitch is a female dog; and then there is the female human being. But there is only one type of woman that the Bible describes beautifully. "Who can find a virtuous woman? for her price is far above rubies. The heart of her husband doth safely trust in her, so that he shall have no need of spoil. She will do him good and not evil all the days of her life.... She openeth her mouth with wisdom; and in her tongue is the law of kindness.... Her children arise up, and call her blessed; her husband also, and he praiseth her" (Prov. 31:10–12, 26, 28). A woman is fully developed, mature, virtuous and pure in nature, relating to the sex that bears the young. When choosing a life partner through the eyes of God, a good Christian man differentiates the character between a woman and a female: he recognizes her tree by the fruit she bears.

Attracting a good Christian man and keeping him takes skills and patience: not sexual skills, but abundant knowledge of the word of God and abiding by His doctrines and teachings.

Mr. Wrong is glamorously wrapped in all sorts of shapes and sizes. There is no particular indicator stamped on his forehead that signals "DANGER! STAY AWAY." But having a relationship with God will allow the Holy Spirit to open our spiritual eyes to look deeply beyond the fleshly surface. Satan's evil tactics to manipulate relationships with lustful desires keeps many females in the dark when it comes to Mr. Right finding them.

About fifty years ago, when there was no such thing as the Internet or a cell phone, relationships seemed to mean more. Meeting a date the old fashioned way almost guaranteed a successful relationship; whereas in the twenty-first century the World Wide Web has made it much easier to locate a potential mate and there is much deception when trying to get to know that mate. For example, when you are sitting alone in front of that lovely computer screen, you can become, create, or portray anyone you like. That is the perfect time to mislead individuals into believing that they have one thing but in fact they have another. Many females are getting caught up in the Internet dating game and later find out that their prince charming was a prince harming. Not all Internet dating ends in failure. There have been many pleasant relationships that started through the Internet and progressed into great marriages. Relationships today appear less grounded than previously, simply because people are living by the world's standards and theories on how they should date.

Men have been stealthily searching for women since biblical times. It's like the old saying, "What a man wants, a man gets." That statement can be either true or false, depending on the situation and circumstances. However, there's no questions asked when a man sees something extremely appealing that he desires to keep forever. If a man truly wants to be with a woman, he will do many things to gain her undivided attention, such as: buying her flowers, taking her on dinner dates, going to the movies, and spending quality time with her. On the other hand, a female should never, by any means, chase a man, especially if he does not want to be caught. The Bible says, "One who finds a wife, finds a good thing" (Prov.

18:22, author's paraphrase), not one who chases behind a man finds a good thing.

When a female puts herself out there on the front lines, it seems to take away that innocence and womanly demeanor. A man knows what he wants, and if he is sending you non-verbal cues that he is not interested, take the hint and move on. It would save you a lot of heartache in the long run. Also, if he does not want you, nothing can make him stay.

Some men appreciate women who allow them to be the man in the relationship. A real man wears the pants and hunts for his prey if he is truly interested. Females should not appear desperate and available when it comes to a good man finding you. Men desire to work for you. Put in the time to gain his trophy so that one day he may look back with delight and enjoy what he has won.

Nevertheless, if you are always waiting near the telephone, sending many text messages throughout the day, showing up at his house unannounced, going to his workplace unannounced, night after night driving by his home, harassing previous girlfriends, and mistakenly showing up at social events where you know he will be, saying that it was coincidental that you both were there, you might never get that man. A host of men will think that you are crazy and need psychotic help; others will believe that they have you on a leash like a female dog.

When a female constantly chases behind a man that is a true sign of desperation and neediness. A woman will not give a man that authority to believe that he is something greater than a man: do not make him an idol god. Females should be positive, confident, and self-assured. Do not continue to be his "standby" or "lady on the side." Women are worthy and deserve to be desired. Let him pursue you.

That is where a flock of females make mistakes. They chase after men who they know very well they cannot have. They are aware that he has his eyes on another prize or that he might already be someone's prize, but females allow themselves to settle behind close doors with him and continue to be his female *fool*. Yes, *fool!* Because that is what we are when we choose to know better but do not live better. Being foolish is lacking discernment and fools invite their own destruction. The Bible states, "For wrath killeth the foolish man, and envy slayeth the silly one" (Job 5:2).

As the old song said, everyone has probably played the fool sometime or another. Just use that experience as a tool to mold your personality into the unique individual you will become, before God sends that special person into your life. From previous personal experience, being a hunter and not the prey was a valuable lesson learned and a wake up call that taught me something rewarding that I can hold dearly to my heart forever. The lesson taught me how to be a woman, not to settle for anything less than the best, be positive, have integrity, know who I am as a person, know that I am worthy, and most of all, I am a child of God, who will give me the desires of my heart. Once I began to change my outlook on life, God sent me a better man; someone who was everything that the man I was chasing was not. When God puts sight to blinded eyes, you can see clearly what was once a picture of darkness.

If you ever want the best out of life, you must consult God in everything you do. There is no other way but God's way and that is the honest truth. There are still good Christian men in the world who are searching for good Christian women to be their wives. Females should not continue to date men when they see no future: everything headed down a dark road. Life is too short to waste time being unhappy.

It is good to date the old-fashioned way—like our grandparents who might still be together after sixty years of marriage. The foundation for a good marriage begins when the couple is dating and become engaged. If you are committed to the person you are dating, then you are more likely to be committed in the marriage.

Before parents allow dating, they should teach and encourage their kids to follow biblical standards rather than worldly standards. Biblical values will help them choose a mate wisely and help them to manage life's difficulties. Troubles and heartache will come, but having biblical standards as a guide will help to ease emotional suffering.

While we are living in this world of sin there will be

calamities. God's Word and teachings help us to deal with and handle stress whenever it arrives. If you wait on God and follow Him, watch how blessed and less stressful life will be.

Reason 2

TOO MUCH PROMISCUOUS SEX AND BED HOPPING

S EX IS A powerful bond that should not be taken lightly. Sexual immorality has no place among Christians and we are to have nothing to do with sexual immorality. God wants everyone to live in holiness, not lustful passion, avoiding those who lead one to fornication.

When a man sleeps around he is considered to be a "player" or a "dog." But when a female sleeps around with many men she is portrayed as a "whore." Society upholds men with great dignity when they are out there having sex with many different women. In God's sight, fornication is fornication, no matter who is committing it.

In today's growing population, where sex is used as if it holds no morals and values, it is hard for some people to abstain from premarital sex with all the sexy advertisements shown on television, billboards, and in magazines. They have even created sexy baby dolls for little girls to play with and cartoon characters for the children to view on TV. It seems like there are only a handful of Christian materials distributed in the marketplace to help people grow spiritually with the Lord and an overwhelming amount of ungodly materials will sure send their souls to eternal death.

Sexual sin begins in the mind and it only takes the thought, desire, and the action to commit fornication. Females do not have to feel validated by sleeping around with men in order to get their stamp of approval. A good Christian man respects a woman when she abstains until they are married. Females should run away with great speed from men who are pressuring them into sex, especially if sex is his main topic of conversation. Most likely, those men are no good. They are just searching for a sexual encounter for the moment.

Many females believe they have to prove themselves by sleeping with a guy who they know does not mean them well. Once the sex is over, what do you have to look forward to? When people go their separate ways after having a one-night stand or a short-term sexual relationship, there will be consequences because of this intimate connection. They may repeat that same mistake by quickly jumping into bed with another partner, without first receiving healing, hoping to fill that space of loneliness.

If a female does meet a good man with the potential for being Mr. Right, she might think her body is the only way to keep his attention. But if he rejects her sexual advances, desiring to wait until he is married, she will probably feel rejected, thinking that something is wrong with him or even herself. Females should cherish their bodies like God intended, staying away from sexual sin that will surely bring negative consequences. Promiscuity destroys the body like a bad disease; it slowly eats into the flesh and leaves behind ugly dark scars.

Health department records indicate that more people are living comfortably with HIV/AIDS and other sexually transmitted diseases as if they are the common cold.[1] Society has made it acceptable by stressing the fact that there are medications and help available to prolong longevity. Yet the wide outbreaks of these distasteful and deadly viruses have not deterred individuals from abstaining from fornication. There are even cases in which mothers with HIV are passing it on to their innocent unborn babies. There are also cheating spouses spreading the disease to their faithful husbands and wives. AIDS has no face and it does not discriminate.

To illustrate, I remember a heart-wrenching story about a deceitful, smooth-talking man who could have seduced any female with his charm and attractive physique. He knew he was good looking and used it to his advantage to lure females into his web of deception. However, he was living a normal sex life with full-blown AIDS and later decided to marry a woman he met without ever disclosing his dirty secret. He purposely engaged in unprotected sexual intercourse with her, hoping that she would get infected so that they could die together. Amazingly, when his secret became public, everyone thought that she had contracted the deadly virus and it would be a matter of time before they both passed away. But what people did not know was that this woman was a child of God, protected by His holy blood, therefore the unclean AIDS blood could not enter into her body.

In another sense, sexual sin will always have negative consequences and a high price to pay. Females who fornicate and then get pregnant do not realize the pressures and burdens that may come along with being a single mother with a child or children. God will help them, but they will still have to suffer the consequences for disobeying His will. But some females fornicate, get pregnant, and try to find an easy way out by having an abortion so that they can move on with their lives as if nothing happened. There is no easy way out because somewhere down the line reaping time will come. God planted that seed into the body for a reason. God forms every child and He cares for the unborn. It would be devastating to a woman who, early on, had an abortion but later on in life desired to have children with her spouse, and then could not because her womb was cursed. That could easily happen and we should be aware that what we do today has a huge impact on tomorrow.

Sex outside of marriage is foolish and society is approving the act without acknowledging the fact that all sin will come to an end. Fornication has consequences, and any female who is willing to share her body with a man who is not her husband does not value herself as a woman. A woman holds back the physical sex allows the man to make love to her mind intellectually so that he can grow to love her unconditionally and see the inner beauty she possesses. She wants to represent the ideal woman that he can take home to meet his family and to some day make his wife.

However, that is not the end of the road for a female who decides to become a woman. She can turn away from wrong doings and make God the head of her life. She can begin to have respect for herself and walk with integrity and to stop being a man's late night friend with benefits. A good Christian man can smell a good Christian woman with self-worth miles away. Men love strong-minded hard-working women who can contribute and stand up for themselves. Your past actions do not have to determine your future. Everyone has sinned and fallen short one time or another. God forgives those who honestly seek Him and live by His will. People who obey God's Word will be blessed.

Moreover, slower is better and there is no need to rush things. If he truly loves you, he will wait until you are his wife before becoming intimate. It is best to wait until the wedding night to give your husband an unopened gift (sex). Sex means so much to a couple if the first time they are intimate with one another is on their wedding night. "Marriage is honourable in all, and the bed undefiled: but whoremongers and adulterers God will judge" (Heb. 13:4).

Sex within marriage is meant to be a delight, very honorable and pure.

Our bodies were not made for sexual immorality. They were made for the Lord, and the Lord cares about our bodies. Don't you realize that our bodies are actually parts of Christ? No other sin so clearly affects the body as this one does. It is like playing Russian Roulette when we engage in sexual sin. There is always a price to pay when we fail to follow God's laws regarding Christian living. God rewards those who wait and keep His commandments.

Reason 3

ENGAGE TO BE ENSLAVED

THERE IS A lot of truth to the old saying, "Why buy the cow when you can get the milk for free?" First of all, cohabitating, "shacking up," or living together—whatever you wish to call it—has become more popular and acceptable in America. God does not ordain common-law marriage, and there is nothing good in it or coming from it. If a man is living with a female, having sex with her, sharing the household bills, and creating a few kids together, more than likely he is not looking forward to taking her down the aisle any time soon.

Society came up with this common-law marriage theory in order to place a fresh label on this type of sin. Although it is not a marriage united under God, it is a marriage assented to by the world that Satan has manipulated into believing it is OK. Why would a female resort to this kind of lifestyle? Does she not know that she is worthy of being someone's wife, placed on a pedestal? Well, the answer to the first question is: she becomes enslaved to her live-in partner's ongoing games. She probably thinks that after five years of living together and having two children together, he will one day marry her. That is the trick of the enemy—a huge deception to deceive the mind in order to control the spirit.

Countless females get stuck in these relationships for years, robbing them of any chance of a good man finding them. Men string females along like dummies, knowing very well that they have no plans for serious commitment. They become enslaved to lame excuses, where the handwriting is clearly written on the wall that these men are just sucking the females' self esteem dry until something more appealing and better comes along.

Have you ever heard or seen where a deadbeat man lives with a female for many years, has kids with her, and then leaves her and marries someone else? If the other female has kids, he may treat those children better than he does his very own. This is why a female should marry before having children. She will have a much better chance of her husband staying with her than if she is just living with him, because there is no commitment involved. Yes, married men leave their wives and children, too, and nothing in the world is guaranteed but the Word of God; but if you both get on one accord with Jesus, the marriage is sure to last a lifetime.

In addition, the kids also suffer in these so-called common law marriages, because where there is no God, there is no peace. God does not live where there is filth and uncleanness. If a teacher ever wants to understand why little Billy, Sally, Tammy, or David are always acting out and are disrespectful in school, she should follow them home one day to discover her answer.

The next answer to the last question is: the female does not feel that she is worthy to be someone's wife because if she did, she would have "put the brakes" on this relationship a long time ago. Love is certainly blind, but it should not make you a fool. Maybe the female feels this way about herself because her live-in man treats her like the gum on the bottom of his shoe. He may verbally ridicule her appearance and her ability to become a woman, enslaving her into thinking that no one else cares and that she cannot excel beyond what he permits. As a result, he may give her a lousy engagement ring: keeping her mind at ease and allowing her to believe that they have a future together. But in fact, that is just another way he continues to control her thoughts and guard her heart with his lock and key.

On the contrary, have you ever met a female who flashes around a beautiful engagement ring on her finger, only to discover that she has been wearing that same ring for ten years or more and has not walked down the aisle yet? The engagement ring should be a symbolic promise to marry when the time is right—hopefully within two years. But to Mr. Wrong, the time is never right. That is his way to dominate and to keep the female tightly secured underneath his belt, subduing her every move.

Females have to feel good about themselves and live

THE FEMALE FOOL

according to God's way, before true love will knock at their door. Mr. Right is not going to come knocking at your front door until you have Mr. Wrong out of the picture. Everything that does not line up with the Word of God is destined for failure. People should do things that honor God. Living without God is living in spiritual darkness.

A good man is not hard to find if God sends him to you. He will be spiritually led into your heart, mind, body, and soul to obtain the goodness that lies within. A Christian dating relationship will lead to a Christian marriage. Therefore, it is right to follow God's Word and do things His way.

Indeed, divorce rates are increasing while the will to live for God is decreasing, because many people are living their lives by the world's standards. The world says it is OK to have children out of wedlock, live together before marriage, and to have sex as long as it feels good. That is why so many homes have now become just houses, with no true meaningful love guided by God's grace and mercy.

Furthermore, females should change their mentality to step up and take control of their lives. Stop being enslaved to a man's weak mind games. A man cannot go further than you allow. So stop getting angry when a Hip-Hop rapper portrays you with very negative images and language in his songs and videos. The bottom line is you can become like a female dog in heat, being controlled on a leash by a man (please excuse my terminology).

The way a female carries herself in public reflects a lot about her character as a person. A Christian man will not want to marry a loud, obnoxious, ill-mannered, trouble-making female who enjoys being heard and seen. If you really want to know who you are as a person, watch what type of people you attract.

Nevertheless, God gives some the gift of marriage, and to others He gives the gift of singleness. But if a female cannot control herself, she should go ahead and marry, not cohabitate, and receive the benefits of a marriage. It is better to marry than to burn with lust. (See 1 Corinthians 7:9.) "Shacking up" is just a cheap way to reap all without giving all. Females can escape from their lover's pathetic chains of life that have their heads all wrapped up with his nonsense. Wake up and smell the coffee. Stop settling and begin setting goals for your life and walk in true happiness the way God designed and love will find you.

Reason 4

CHANGE YOUR WAY
OF THINKING
Renew your mindset—renew your heart

OUR MINDS AS human beings and the natural way we think began long before we could ever speak a single word. The way a pregnant mother nurtures her womb determines what will birth out of it. For example, if you would like to eat a good tasting chocolate cake you must add the right ingredients. A bad tasting cake has bad ingredients. If a child grows up to be bad, he probably had bad ingredients used to make him. Perhaps both parents and a generation of his family members are spiritually disconnected from God. "Either make the tree good, and his fruit good; or else make the tree corrupt, and his fruit corrupt: for the tree is known by his fruit" (Matt. 12:33).

To raise up a child in a relationship with God is the best gift a parent could ever give their kids. What we learn as children has a lot to do with how we think and handle life decisions as adults. The brain is a terrible thing to waste and what we instill into the mind sometimes manifests into the heart. For instance, many girls may grow up with the mentality that it is OK for a female to be dominated, controlled, abused, lied to, or cheated on by a man because she observed from home her mother, aunts, cousins, or other relatives living their lives in that manner. Her subconscious minds take notes, preparing her for the day she could become the next doormat underneath a deadbeat man's feet. But God says, "Walk in the spirit and you will not fulfill the lust of the flesh" (Gal. 5:16). Walking in the Spirit is a way of thinking that lines up with the Word of God. Walking in the flesh is a way of thinking that is in opposition to the Word of God.

A myriad of females are attracting the wrong kind of men simply because of the way they are thinking. If a female thinks she can take another woman's husband, change the behavior of a man, thinks she is God's greatest gift to all men, thinks she can get him to love her, or thinks that it is OK to live by the world's standards, she is headed toward failure.

Your mindset determines your life set. The things that are in your head will decide your future. You cannot control the future, yet you can control the treasures in your heart and that will determine your future. "A good man out of the good treasure of the heart bringeth forth good things: and an evil man out of the evil treasure bringeth forth evil things" (Matt. 12:35).

Our fellowship with God helps us to make right

decisions and we should please God with our thoughts. Females can live in harmony with their soul mates if they put God first and live by His words. You cannot think like the world and expect to have greatness for your life. It will not last or remain. Have an attitude of joy, love, gladness, honor, and thanksgiving because your attitude will determine your altitude: how high you will go in life. Do not let the devil have victory over your future.

If you would like to change your life and wish for a good man to find you, you must change your mindset on how you view men or you will continue to attract that same type of man. You must renew your mind and thoughts into God's thoughts. Change requires you to desire to change and a decision to change. You have to think differently and disassociate yourself from negative atmospheres. Pray for discernment to acknowledge what is real and unreal. Mr. Wrong comes in all shapes, sizes, and colors. But it is discernment that will unveil his character.

Furthermore, females have to learn to think right or Satan will deceive their minds. That is how a lot of females get stuck in a rut with the wrong men. They fail to learn that there is more to a man than what they see. What the female may see is a strong, muscular, good looking outer shell, who drives a fancy sporty car, lives at home with his sister, has a wallet full of money, and has a great nighttime job. But what they do not see is that the car he is driving is not his, he lives at home with his wife, and at night he hustles in the streets as a drug dealer bringing in a lot of money. "And Jesus answered and said unto them, Take heed that no man deceive you" (Matt. 24:4).

When the devil wants your mind, he will fill it up with lies and misconceptions in order to get you off point. You should pray to overcome his treacherous tactics to lure souls. Prayer is a spiritual weapon that is used to fight off the enemy. Prayer should be our first line of defense, which opens doors for God to come in and work.

To reiterate, we as people can control what we think. You can make yourself miserable with your own thoughts, and everyday should be endured with positive thinking and motivation. We have to think with the mind of the spirit not with the mind of the head. Today, the reason why so many people are in critical predicaments is due to living by the world's system: if it does not look right to the mind of the flesh, it must not be right.

Everyday life stresses from this struggling economy have taken a swarm of souls to the grave because they allowed their mind of the flesh to control the spirit. The world says that everyone is in hard times: a famine among the land. But God's Word says, "Trust in the LORD with all thine heart; and lean not unto thine own understanding" (Prov. 3:5–6). It is God's will for man to prosper. "And be not conformed to this world: but be ye transformed by the renewing of your mind, that ye may prove what is that good and acceptable, and perfect, will of God" (Rom. 12:2).

Primarily, females should cease from thinking that they have a certain type of man in mind to date, because a man who might not be their type could very well be Mr. Right. To illustrate, there is nothing wrong with having a preference when choosing a lifetime partner. But some females go overboard as if they were born looking like a beautiful queen without flaws. They think they must have the best looking man, incredible body, highly educated, and a certain skin tone. Sadly, many females have lost out on good Christian men simply because he was not light, dark, smart, physically fit enough, or he didn't have the right job title, live in the right house, or drive the right model vehicle. Satan has swindled the world into believing that you cannot live off love alone and that material gains equal much success. Love cannot pay the bills, but it sure will feel good to lie beside love in a matchbox and know that it is genuine, and full of God's grace from the heart.

Thus, once females plant the seed in their minds and speak that they are somebody and will not accept anything the world has to offer, good things will blossom because there is power, life, and death in the words we say. Words affect the soul and the spirit. Whatever is happening in the soul and spirit are manifesting in the heart. When you change your thinking, you change your life.

Reason 5

GOLD DIGGER, MONEY TRIGGER

IRST AND FOREMOST, I would like to give you the definition of a gold digger from the world's point of view. A gold digger is nothing but a lazy person who preys on the opposite sex for money. They enter into relationships for material benefits, knowing very well that when the money is gone, so are they. Gold diggers do not value dating. They view relationships like a business transaction and do not care who gets hurt in the process.

A *woman* does not possess gold digging tendencies—only the female and sometimes deadbeat men. Gold diggers think that it is cute to have a "sugar daddy" or a "sugar mama" paying all their bills and supporting their gold-digging habits. Some men dread the thought of dating a gold digger yet other men embrace it. A gold digger is nothing but an uncovered prostitute. The only difference between the two is that a prostitute works for her money and a gold digger does not.

Some females allow deadbeat men to live off their hard-earned money while they are the ones getting up in the morning, going to work as the man sleeps until noonday, and later invites all of his unemployed friends over for a card game, munching on and eating up all the food in your refrigerator, and then having the audacity to get mad at you for coming home early. She allows this attitude because she is weak-minded and believes she has to keep supporting this male gold digger in order to keep him around. Many females think that they cannot handle things by themselves: misery always loves company.

Deadbeat men seek after successful females who appear to have it all together financially but not emotionally. They are well trained in their skillful, manipulative minds to scout out these types of females by the way they converse within the first few minutes of meeting them. They know right from the beginning if she is a good candidate to be suckered for her money. When a female first starts using negative words in the conversation—it could be about herself, weather, the environment, past relationships, family members or friends—he knows instantly she has some emotional issues. A mature, confident woman is not going to speak negatively about anything when first meeting someone. She has high standards and likes the opposite sex to acknowledge those standards by speaking positively, with only godly thoughts guiding the conversation. Deadbeat men run away from strong, grounded women who have the common sense to know a snake by the way it looks. She does not have to be bitten in order to know he exists.

A cloud of females live their lives this way and think that it is OK to date low-life men who are not contributing to the relationship. She tolerates the man and allows him to drive her nice car around town, and then discovers that her car is being parked in another female's driveway. Better yet, he is driving around the neighborhood with the other female in her vehicle. He does not show her respect because he knows she did not have the backbone to toss him out, therefore, he continues to spend her money and suck all the life out of her until she is not fit to meet a good man with potential, who will treat her like a real woman, someone who will not take anything from her but who will make her the special mate that God designed.

Money can create the worst-case scenario when it is mishandled and used for ungodly purposes. "Lay not up for yourself treasures upon earth, where moth and rust doth corrupt, and where thieves break through and steal" (Matt. 6:19). Money can buy all the material things in the world but one thing it cannot buy is happiness. What good is it to gain riches and wealth and then die and lose your soul? (See Mark 8:36.) The answer is: nothing. You cannot take anything to the grave with you anyway. Money can distract people from God if they are allowing the money to make them, instead of them making the money; you cannot serve both God and money. Greed brings on trouble and destruction, and we should always look to God for security, not money. People who are full of greed will not enter heaven. "For this ye know, that no whoremonger, nor unclean person, nor covetous man, who is an idolater, hath any inheritance in the kingdom of Christ and of God" (Eph. 5:5).

In a like manner, the reason why some females cannot attract a good Christian man is because they are gold diggers too. Many females live their lives destructively when they pursue men only for their money and what they can do for them. A woman works hard to earn money, appreciating her God-given talents and strengths to succeed without the help from a man. On the other hand, females would rather take the easy route in life and depend on men for their lap of luxury, and by the time they are old, their bodies are not physically fit anymore to keep up with the changing world. She has nothing or no one to share her later years with, because she used her entire youthfulness playing mind games with men and using them for the money.

If females continue to allow gold-digging men to sucker them out of their earnings, they will always be financially stable fools, never knowing how good Christian men would treat them. Also, if a female keeps nurturing her gold-digging lifestyle by dating established men only for their money, destruction is sure to follow. Not only will she not meet a good Christian man, but she also might attract the wrong kind of man who will not take it lightly that he is being suckered out of his money. To give an example, I remember a young college female from a number of years ago who had everything to live for. However, she met a man and thought she could use him for his money while in college and then dump him once she graduated. But sadly, things did not progress that way. He was a drug dealer and did not take kindly to being played like a fool for his money. He supported her monetarily all the way through college and when she graduated, she dumped him as planned. Then one day, unexpectedly, he viciously ran her down in public and shot her dead.

Sin has consequences and it leads to eternal death. God will punish sin and He is willing to forgive our transgressions if we ask with a sincere spirit. Sin begins in the mind and our conscience can identify sin. As stated before, a female should carry herself like a woman with the utmost respect that is pleasing to God. A gold digger's reputation will follow her throughout life. Men will recognize her for what she is and the only way to escape that harmful past is to turn away from all wrongdoing and repent of all sin. Repentance of sin opens the way for a relationship with God.

But, the world is not too easy to forgive and forget. Every chance they get, they will remind you of what wrong you have done previously, ignoring the new shield that God has transformed. Many gossiping people love to bring up others' wrong doings while forgetting that they, too, have skeletons in their closet that have not been buried. They stroll around town and converse about everyone as if they were born sin-free. The best way to handle negativity when it is tossed in your face is to throw it down and stomp it underneath your foot. If they cannot make you, by all means, they cannot break Money is good to have if God gives it to you. The devil also gives away money, but we should be mindful of how we obtain and use our money. Gold diggers have no rewarding future unless their activity ceases. A successful woman who knows what she wants out of life does not have to play on a man's emotions just to get inside his wallet. Success takes hard work, dedication, and determination. There is nothing more appealing to a Christian man than to see a successful Christian woman living her life for God. Therefore, females should walk with probity and guard their reputation from sinful actions. A good reputation can be built by obeying God's Word.

Reason 6

STOP BEING THE 1ˢᵗ OF THE MONTH FEMALE

GOVERNMENTAL BENEFITS ARE very helpful to people who are truly in desperate need of assistance. If they suddenly become unemployed, have physical and mental disabilities, are elderly, or are a widowed mother who lost the breadwinner in the home, these benefits would come in handy. But what about females who are having illegitimate babies out of wedlock, abusing the welfare system for their own monetary gains? They apply for food stamps and welfare checks, manipulating the agency as if every cent will be spent for food and the needs for which the check is intended.

But if only the government could be a fly on the wall, they would recognize how these females trade their food stamps for a couple of dollars, use the welfare checks for hair styling, clothing, manicures, pedicures and to take care of their no good boyfriends, who are probably living with them in their section eight duplex that the government is supplying.

A young, single female with kids can receive help from the government more quickly than an elderly woman who has contributed to society and honestly earned her wages throughout life. Females think that it is an easy way of life to have to depend on the government for help. Having kids before you can take care of them is stupidity. Some females do make the first mistake and get caught up in the moment, fall for the wrong man, and then have his baby. But to continue to this pattern with non-Christian men and have several of their kids is not acceptable. They knew what type of man he was before having sex with him and now he is probably with another female, in jail, or nowhere to be found. He goes off and leaves them with the children, and more likely creating more kids that he is not going to acknowledge and support, repeating the same thing. The children sometimes suffer from this because now they might be raised in a single-parent home without a father, where all of their siblings have different last names.

Females should think about their future before engaging in sexual practices that are truly against the will of God. Thirty minutes of pleasure is not worth the lifetime of pain that comes after giving birth to a child that will probably not get to know their real father. The children never asked to be here and all kids should know who their parents are. Females have unprotected sex and bear children with men who they know have one or more "baby mamas." He did not marry them, what makes you think he will marry you? He is just a weekend father or a monthly child support check.

Many females sleep around with different men, get pregnant and then don't know who impregnated them. They go on national television to establish paternity, exposing their sex life with two or more men, hoping to earn their fifteen minutes of fame. Actually, it is fifteen minutes of shame, because not only are the men disgracing them before millions, but also, she is disgracing herself and her babies.

The Bible speaks of fornication and bearing children out of wedlock. Children are a blessing from God, but they should be created from a husband and a wife. A virtuous woman with a keen mind, protected by God's mercy, can sense a "player" or a "dog" in heat when he is trying to seduce her. Though a female cannot recognize the game, even if she thinks she can. She is blinded with deception in the hopes of satisfying her flesh.

If a female did make a mistake and went down the wrong path in life and had a child or children out of wedlock, she still has time to turn things around and become the woman God designed. It is not where you have been that determines success; it is where you are going. There have been many, many women who got involved with the wrong men and had their babies, but they did not allow their past misfortunes to dictate their futures. They have gone on to live for God, prosper with good careers and have settled into good marriages.

God does not stigmatize or place identification slips on people just because they make mistakes. He gives us all choices to make our own decisions. We should ask God for wisdom before making decisions. But God does not make us do anything, the choice remains with us. We can choose to live, or we can choose to die. God's teachings are there for us if we desire to accept it.

Females can decide to stand firm and obey God's Word to obtain excellence in their lives. Stop being the first of the month female and seek a better way. Stop allowing the government to take care of you and your kids. There is nothing good about the government telling you what you can buy and where to buy it. Obtaining welfare checks and food stamps should only apply to the needy that honestly need the assistance or meet certain requirements that prohibit them from working. Hard work is valued and laziness can make you poor. "He becometh poor that dealeth with a slack hand: but the hand of the diligent maketh rich" (Prov. 10:4).

Reach for the stars and be all that God says you can be. The way a woman intellectually speaks her mind, uses her skills to honor God, and acknowledges what she wants in her future guided by God's grace and mercy, will attract a good Christian man more speedily than her fleshly outer appearance.

SPIRITUALLY DISCONNECTED

THERE ARE SO many unsaved people living in the world believing that they have all the time left to get their soul right with God. But no one knows the time, hour, or day that his or her life will end. God says, "Be ye ready." Death is a result of sin and every person will face death. But do not get caught dead without God, because if you do, the outcome is more excruciating than any other pain that exists.

Just imagine being locked down in a burning house, feeling the overbearing heat stripping your flesh from your naked bones, only to discover that there will never, ever be fire departments, rescue missions, or anyone available to put out the flames. Hell is a place of eternal fire, where God will send people who chose to live their lives without Him. When you refuse to walk by the Word of God, you are living in spiritual darkness and are spiritually disconnected from God. God can save anyone from everlasting darkness if they would give Him their heart.

On the flipside, people desire to have the favor of

God over their lives, but do not want to live the way he requires. They seek Him only when they are in trouble, sickness comes upon their bodies, or they need a special prayer request. This is why the world is in such turmoil with a lot of pain and suffering. If everyone would turn away from unrighteous living and humble himself or herself in Christ, the world would be an awesome place to live.

However, when it comes to choosing a life partner, it is best for both to be spiritually connected: not unequally yoked. But if a female happens to fall in love and marry an unsaved man before she becomes a woman, she can witness to her non- Christian husband in hopes to bringing him to Christ. Many females fail to see what is clearly stated before becoming involved with a man. It is impossible to meet a good Christian man without first meeting God. Satan paints pretty pictures just to deceive the mind. Females should pray for a husband, not just a man. They should pray for a husband with the heart for God.

The Lord will bless a female with a good Christian man if she so desires. But first, she has to be willing to change her lifestyle and her mindset and that comes with much sacrifice and obedience. When you develop a strong relationship with God and begin to see things for what they truly are, wisdom and knowledge of His presence manifests that will exemplify nobility that will last a lifetime. People should crave from the heart to do things that are pleasing to God. When you start to seek Jesus from the deep pits of your soul that is when you see steps in your life change for the best.

Indeed, it is so important to acquire a relationship with Christ before one marries. Husband and wife need to be spiritually whole, growing closer to God together. The reason why numerous marriages end in divorce is because of unrealistic expectations not aligned with what God says. First of all, they settle into a relationship God had no intention of fulfilling. Now, after a few years of marriage, the couple is miserable, depressed, grouchy, unhappy, and tries to find other means (besides turning to God) to make the marriage work, only to find themselves standing in front of a judge ending a sacred bond that was never confirmed by God. Marriage is not a one man's show. It takes three to make a marriage work: God, the husband, and the wife.

Society has redefined how marriages should be. Some people are not marrying for the sake of love, and whoever would have thought that same-sex marriages would be approved? Or, better yet, acknowledged in a land that was truly built on the foundation of God. A marriage should embed sacrificial love from its roots, created upon the Word of God. In the family, everything starts with the husband, the head of his household, just as Christ is the head of all things. Specifically, if a husband has not submitted himself to Christ, he has no right to tell his wife to submit to him.

In another manner, some people are crying spiritually because they are confining themselves spiritually to fit the form of society. We, as Christians, live in the world, but are not of the world. We do not follow their example; we set the example. Having a personal intimate relationship with God means we should include Him in our daily life. We should pray, attend church, read the Bible, meditate on scriptures, and listen to inspirational materials, because all of these items are efforts to get to know Him. The Holy Spirit has been given to us as our Teacher, "If you love me, you will obey what I command" (John 14:15).

Spiritual connections show signs that we possesses a deep connection to God, which will allow Him to work in our lives. There is no such thing as a perfect relationship without God. The Lord helps us to grow spiritually, and we should separate ourselves from the world's point of view. The world has no connections to God and has done its best to disassociate Him from everything.

In short, when a female is spiritually connected to God, she will fully grow into maturity, acquiring all she can to transform into an exemplary woman, guided by the Holy Spirit that will empower her to be ready when a good Christian man comes along. They that wait on the Lord shall inherit his blessings. What God ordains you will maintain.

Reason 8

LOW SELF-ESTEEM

OVER THE YEARS, the way society has defined beauty has inflicted more self-doubt into females. Popular, upscale magazines and television programs portray attractiveness as wearing nothing larger than a size three with white or light-skinned faces. Our image plays a major role in the world that makes it uneasy for others to accept who they are as an individual, always wanting to look or be something they are not. That is how jealousy and envy grow throughout the body like cancer and later destroy every cell that God has formed.

We are made in God's image, created by Him in His own special way. Humankind has been formed by God's loving hands and is of great value. We should never over or under estimate ourselves. Our self-esteem is affected by our relationship with Christ and His approval is the only one that matters. When the favor of God is over your life, no one or nothing can stop what God has planned. It does not matter whose body is the slimmest or whose face the prettiest. If God says, "I want this two hundred pound, ugly woman with bad hair and leathery skin gracing the cover of this well-known magazine, then my word will be done." The reason we have not seen a swarm of these types of faces in the spotlight is because we, as people, do not believe it could happen. There is power and life in the words we say. God will perform the same supernatural miracles he did back then, but our faith has declined tremendously, as our minds are so wrapped tightly into what the eyes see, instead of what the spirit believes.

In another sense, females who permit men to negatively change who they are as a person to satisfy his own fleshly ego, have some self-esteem issues. Women walk in excellence and are all they can be regardless of how the world views them. Females need to cease changing themselves for a man and learn to love what they see in the mirror. Everyone cannot look like a fashion doll, be a perfect size six, or have the nicest skin, but we can appreciate what we have it and use it to the fullest to make it presentable to the eyes of the most highest.

Conversely, females who possess low self-esteem may fall for anything and any line that a guy throws at them. She tends to sleep around with men who only acknowledge her at night or behind closed doors. She is the one who will never get to meet his mother, his friends, or be seen with him in the public. He knows she has issues and uses it to his advantage to get what he wants when he wants it. It is sad to see a man deceive a female in this cruel manner. But the world says you cannot fault the man for being a man. The female has to take responsibility and safeguard her heart against treacherous acts like this. Females have been living under the illusion that what they look like, type of job they have, their educational level, where they live, and how well they can use their bodies in bed with men, are the only ways to acquire a meaningful relationship. They need to realize that materialistic values and physical beauty do not measure their self-worth.

Additionally, low self-esteem is keeping females from a serious Christian relationship with decent men. If she does not feel good about herself, then she will think no one else will. Having low self-esteem also affects other areas in life where depression, anxiety, loneliness, and discouragement take hold in the mind. In order to gain self-esteem, she must know that God accepts her for who she is. Many females who suffer from low self-esteem have had negative past experiences that have taken a toll on them. It may have begun in childhood or adulthood. They fear being undesirable and will not take risks that involve failure. Fear like this keeps females from attracting good Christian men, and they often fall into the arms of abusers, cheater, liars, etc.

We must understand that, in Christ, past failures and experiences do not occupy our lives anymore. We must believe in ourselves and be happy. Avoid negativity and old habits that bring upon self-doubt. Smile everyday and give God the thanks for waking you up this morning.

Learn something new each day that will empower and open up your heart to grow spiritually as a person. Learn to love without pulling from the past. Yesterday is gone—a distant memory. Today starts a new beginning while tomorrow remains a mystery. Learn to have inner peace by ignoring the things you have no control over and let God handle the rest. Have a mindset to enjoy each moment because every second of your life counts for something and every second lost can never be regained.

Good self-esteem only comes with a real relationship from God. Females should accept their imperfections and love the skin they are in. Stop comparing yourself to other females, and if a man does not desire to have you the way you are, then he is not the one for you. Stop allowing a man to physically and verbally abuse you. It is not right for a man to hit a female; nor is it right for him to belittle her character. She should not live her life for him and stay in a relationship when she knows very well that it is toxic, poisonous, and bad for her health. She always thinks that the man will change but honestly, sometimes he does not. The majority of the time it gets worse and turns into something drastic and detrimental.

Females with self-esteem issues can pray for God to rebuild their confidence and strive to be the best. Prayer is very powerful and it is our communication to connect with God. Christ hears the prayers of the humble and it is hard to be knocked, torn, or slapped down when you are already on your knees. The Lord's strength can give us courage to defeat all things that come against our will to live for Him.

In another manner, females with low self-esteem tend to dress provocatively and work in degrading industries such as: pornography, exotic dancers, prostitution, and personal escorts in order to gain attention from men. A decent woman will not allow men to exploit her sexually for their own sexual pleasures. Some females feel as though they have to resort to these types of jobs in order to make ends meet and for years get caught up in the "quick-money" lifestyle, only obtaining educational skills on how to be the best half-dressed groupie. They have no shame in their game. In fact, females who go to this length to look good for men send a message that they are an easy target and crave the attention. If a female desires to attract a good Christian man, to him it is not what you reveal, it is what you hide that will captivate his mind.

I have learned through TV, the Internet, books, newspapers and magazines that there are many females these days, over the age of fifty, who remain single. They have not found a man to share their life. The truth is that a multitude of females are not living their lives the way God requires. You cannot continue to disobey His Word and expect things to go well in life. People know that fornication is wrong but they continue to do it anyway, and then expect God to work out a miracle if they happen to contract AIDS while going against His will. Or, they happen to become pregnant and know that the father is not going to be around. Some of us set our own fate and fall into destruction simply because we chose to do things our way. When you continue to be disobedient to Christ that displeases Him and before long, he takes His loving hands of guidance from over your life and then Satan steps in and takes control.

In contrast, females should not keep being a fool for a man. What is more sickening to hear is when a foolish female believes everything a man has to say. For instance, many deadbeat men love to play "missing in action" when they want to run around with a lot of females and do not wish to be seen with her in the public. At night, he is at your house, wining and dining you with sweet words of affection and having sex with you, but soon as morning arrives, he quickly leaves your house before daybreak. All during the day, you are calling his cell phone only to receive his voice mail, you are driving by his apartment and sees his car parked in the driveway, but he is not answering the doorbell, you call all of his close family members and friends but they have not seen him either. But as soon as nighttime falls again, he surprisingly appears unannounced at your home late in the midnight hour with lame excuses as to his daytime whereabouts, and the female fool believes him.

Thus, as stated previously, females who are unsure of themselves will fall for anything. They need to allow the love of God to manifest in their hearts and know what they do for Him is good enough. You need to fight to regain your self-esteem. Always think positive and make progress in your life. The devil is the one who embeds negative thinking and holds you from achieving all that God desires. What a person thinks so is he. Good Christian men hunt for women who are self-assured and know how to handle their business with God as their spectator.

THE MARRIED-MAN SYNDROME
Someone who cheats with will cheat on

MARRIAGE IS A holy and sacred bond united by God to join a man and a woman together until death do them part. There is no room for a third party; therefore, no one should come between a husband and a wife. Yet some men are not cherishing their wedding vows and are committing adultery with females just to satisfy the lust of the flesh. Adultery has consequences and it is one of the Ten Commandments, "Thou shalt not commit adultery" (Exod. 20:14).

There are many females who prefer to date married men because they feel as though the behavior is exciting and risky. A married man is totally off-limits and females who submit to these men are depriving themselves of achieving a good Christian man whom they can call their own. However, many females fall victim to the number one deceitful luring tactic by these married men who might say, "My wife does not make me happy anymore. I am just there for the kids." But, just because she plays the victim to his lies and schemes, that does not give her the right to pursue him.

Likewise, females who share their bodies with married men lack self-worth and assurance. Some of these females are young and naïve, easily deceived by men who have years of experience playing manipulative mind games for their own sexual gratification. Not all home-wrecking females are young at heart, but also there are many old females age thirty and above who are chasing after married men who they know very well is someone else's private property.

There are many reasons why females are in hot pursuit of married men. *To begin*, they do not think anyone will find out. It is like the old saying, "What you don't know can't hurt you." The female feels that as long as no one knows, she is not doing anything wrong, and it is OK to continue this relationship until something leaks out and the situation breaks loose. God sees all and knows all. There is nothing so dark and hidden under the sun that He is not aware of. God will let a bird fly so high and when it is time for him to come down, he falls down.

Secondly, she is afraid of commitment. The female desires someone who is already attached and committed. She does not have to carry around all the problems of a husband that the wife does. She can borrow him whenever she likes and then send him back home when she is done. There are no strings attached.

Third, the female enjoys the competition and the excitement that may come along with dating a married man. She views him as a prize and is challenged to triumph if he leaves his wife for her. But what she fails to realize is that her prize has already been won. He made vows to his wife for a lifetime.

Fourth, she needs to feel desired. Many of the females who engage in these types of relationships feel like they can gain power, authority, and confidence by sleeping around with high-profile men or any man who shows them attention. This is how they gain energy to build up low self-esteem that was probably torn down from past broken relationships.

Fifth, he offers monetary benefits that can pay her bills. The female might be a gold digger, on welfare, in college, or just having a hard time making ends meet. She continues to be his mistress on the side for a short time or as long as her needs are being fulfilled.

Sixth, the female is jealous of his wife and family. She sees the man that she wants with a beautiful wife and kids on his arm. They may live in a very nice neighborhood with a fine house. He treats his wife like a queen and the female gets envious and goes after this man, hoping to receive that same affection he shows his wife. She later discovers that he will never leave his wife and that she was only his late-night rendezvous.

Seventh, she is lonely due to past failed relationships. Females who prefer to date married men have low self-esteem and desire a little boost to jump-start their lives. Females have been living with the mentality that they need a man to feel validated. In past relationships, it could have ended badly, where their hearts are left empty and cold, and now they cannot keep a man of their own. They may feel the need to take something that does not belong to them. They are unable to trust again, and they safeguard their feelings by sleeping around with attached men, which will create more drama if they ever fall in love with them.

And finally, the female is sexually attracted to the married man. The man might be sexy, handsome, and very appealing to the eyes. She knows that he is married and only wishes to be intimate with him because the intimacy is tempting. They have an understanding that the relationship is purely based on sex and he has no intentions of leaving his wife. She has no problem with the plan until one day, after twenty years of sleeping with this man, she looks in the mirror and actually realizes where the time has gone. She is now forty years old, has no kids and no one she can call her own.

What makes a female a fool for a married man is her inability to understand that if he cheats on his wife, it's more than likely he will cheat on her. Why do they think that they are much better than the one who he stood with before God and made a promise to be faithful until death do them part? They are nothing special to him: just a quick piece of action when he desires it. Yes, there are some married men who do leave their wives and then marry their mistresses, but the list is very short. If a wife happens to divorce her husband after an adulterous affair, more than likely he is not going to run back into the arms of the female that caused him to get the divorce.

Similarly, females should stay away from married men who say that they are separated from their wives. While they might be separated and both living their lives as single individuals, in God's eyes the two are still married and if the female engages in an intimate relationship with him, he has committed adultery and they will suffer the consequences for such actions. No one knows where death is and it would be sorrowful for one to die while sinning. There have been many cases where spouses, their lovers, or both of them were found dead in hotel rooms, parks etc.

I can recall a story about a man and a female who were both married to other people but were having an adulterous affair. They would leave their hometown in their own vehicles and meet up in another city, leave one car parked in a public parking lot and pair up to drive away to another city to get a hotel room. But sadly, on their way to the hotel, they were tragically killed in a car accident. Another incident I remember dealt with a cheating elderly man found dead in a hotel room. Apparently, he had suffered a heart attack and was left to die alone.

The mistress quickly vacated the scene after calling the paramedics.

God allows sin to go so far until He gets tired and removes His hands of mercy. When God's shield of protection is no longer guiding your pathway, Satan comes in and does what he does best: steal, kill, and destroy. God loves everyone and He wants all to experience a home in heaven when we die and leave this sinful world. Time is winding down and there is no time for foolishness. Sin is pleasurable only for a moment. It has a due season where it, too, will come to an end.

Above all, God is very forgiving and will forgive anyone for his or her sins. A female who violated another woman by sleeping with her husband can turn her life around by doing what is right. Your past transgressions do not determine who you are once you give your life to Christ. Do not worry about what the outside world says. Yes, people will try to condemn a female for being a home wrecker, but if they walk by the spirit of God, those comments will bounce off them like a basketball.

A married man who is willing to cheat on his wife is nothing but a coward. He cannot be a real man if he does not stand up and challenge those issues he is having with his wife or himself. Females should stop being his play toy during the day and his mistress at night. Females deserve a chance to become women, the way God intended. There are good Christian men in this world that make potential mates. But, the females have to let go of the married man and allow God to clean up their life in order to have an open mind. Once the Lord renews their mindset, they will begin to see the world in a brand new way that will bring more joy, happiness, and peace to their life.

Reason 10

ACCEPT THAT IT IS OVER
The Thrill Is Gone

FALLING IN LOVE is such a strong, wonderful, and warm feeling that should connect two hearts together to create an everlasting bond that no man can tear apart. But sometimes one falls out of love and they can no longer mend together the broken pieces of glass, which held so much passion. This may leave the other partner extremely distraught. Breaking up and leaving a somewhat committed relationship is never easy and should be managed with great sincerity and compassion, because the heart is a very fragile, delicate fragment of flesh that does not always deal well with pain.

Some people, who are insanely driven by the thoughts of reciprocation, where the love between the two is now not mutual, and they cannot accept the fact that the relationship is over. They become evil spirited and go great measures in order to gain that person back, but in fact, they are pushing that individual further away with their overbearing demeanor.

Perhaps many of us have encountered in our lives a love stricken boyfriend or girlfriend who was not willing to let us go without first putting up a fight. There once was a period in society when couples could break up peacefully and go their separate ways without chaos and drama. Currently, times have changed for the worst and so many relationships end violently, where someone goes to jail for domestic violence or someone goes to the morgue from a homicide. Selfish, undeniable love can make an unsaved soul do vile things that he would not have done if his life were grounded by the Word of God. Love is a priceless gift that should never be fulfilled only for self-satisfaction. Love should be sacred, cherished, and abided within the heart because love lives forever in places where it is appreciative.

On the flipside, females who cannot or will not accept that a rancid relationship is over leave no room in their inner circle for true love to enter. Many females say with their mouths that they have gotten over an ex-boyfriend, but their actions speak differently if they happen to see that same ex boyfriend with another female. In order to attain a fresh outlook on life, they cannot keep pulling pain from your past. There is a reason why he became their ex and they must accept that it is over and move on with life. They must let go of the emotional baggage that causes biting nails, weight gain, hair loss, dark circles around the eyes, depression, closing off socially from the world, and worst of all, closing themselves off from God.

Do not continue to chase waterfalls. It can keep you from developing new profound relationships. Redirect your attention elsewhere; go out with family and friends, stop communicating with him, delete him off your list of computer friends, tear up old photos of you two together, and occupy your leisure time with a hobby and sooner or later, you will not be thinking about him. Just learn from the lesson and reflect on it as his loss and another man's gain.

Females can decide to make God the center of their souls and receive a brand new beginning. Every day is a new beginning in God. Do not let condemnation take over your will power to receive the plan that the Lord has for you. Be all you can be and never give up on success. You will be amazed what can happen when you persevere and move on to greater tasks. All things are possible with Christ. No matter what you may come up against, never say, "I can't."

Words are powerful and the tongue can destroy. Be determined and do not waste your precious time in life doing nothing. Everyone has a purpose for being in this world. It is mainly up to you to discover what that purpose is. Whenever you start something meaningful, complete it no matter how hard or difficult it may be. It will not be easy but it will be worth it in the long run.

For example, there was a young lady who desired to attend college but no one believed that she was capable enough to attend. She knew deeply that she was and that she had the potential to do anything she set her heart to do. Negativity was not going to stop what God had in store for her life. Along the way, there were many horrible stumbling blocks that attempted to get her off track, but she had the taste and appetite for greatness, which kept her feet on solid ground.

The lady said that she prayed to the Lord on bended knees and made Him a promise that she *would* graduate from college no matter how long it took. Amazingly, not only did she graduate from college, but also she went on to graduate school and received a master's degree that no one would have expected.

In another manner, God helps those who first help themselves. Nothing in the world is free but salvation, and many people find that hard to achieve. If a female would like a better life and she is tired of doing the same old things that are not getting results, she can learn to love herself and she will be able to love others. She should detach herself from old habits that have strongholds over her future. She can break free with the Lord's magnificent love. If there are any strongholds in her pathway that keep her chained down to the past, I recommend these Bible verses for relief:

> For the weapons of our warfare are not carnal, but mighty through God to the pulling down of strong holds.
>
> —2 CORINTHIANS 10:4

read

> Stand fast therefore in the liberty wherewith
> Christ hath made us free, and be not entangled
> again with the yoke of bondage.
>
> —GALATIANS 5:1

Remember, sin has no use for you once its work is
completed. It uses your soul just like a short-term sexual
relationship uses your body.

My Mighty Good Man

By: Melissa Diane Hudson

My one and only Man full of grace,
love to look at His handsome face.
The One that every man wishes he could be,
there is only one like Him can't you see.
He moves my spirit and enlightens my day,
He does it daily in His own special way.
He cradles and rocks me until I fall asleep,
He is truly the One I will always keep.
His strong arms are like pillows; you can rest well
    on Him throughout the night,
He will comfort, hold, and embrace you so tight.
His voice is so harmonizing, very manly and
    pleasing to the ears,
He speaks to me not at me, been this way all of
    these years.
He is forever there for me during the good times
    and the bad,
He is the best man I've ever had.
He's never cheated, lied, or abused this lovely
    temple,
His love is unconditional, proving it is very simple.
When He touches my soul, it sets my heart on
    fire,

this Man is terrific, awesome, the only One my
heart will ever desire.
Every female and woman should want this good
Christian Man in their life,
His first name is Jesus and last name is Christ.

TODAY I CELEBRATE MY LOVE.

Set me as a seal upon thine heart, as a seal upon
thine arm: for love is strong as death; jealousy is
cruel as the grave: the coals thereof are coals of
fire, which hath a most vehement flame.

—SONG OF SONGS 8:6

NOTES

Reason 2

1. From Centers for Disease Control report, "Diagnoses of HIV Infection and AIDS in the United States and Dependent Areas, 2009; HIV Surveillance Report, Volume 21" from website: http://www.cdc.gov/hiv/surveillance/resources/reports/2009report/ (accessed March 1, 2011).

ABOUT THE AUTHOR

MELISSA DIANE HUDSON has a Master's degree in Education from Troy University and a Bachelor's degree in psychology from Albany State University. She has been a guest on *The Montel Williams Show* and was featured in the April 2006 issue of *International Women* magazine. She is a widow and lives in Albany, Georgia, with her son.

CONTACT THE AUTHOR

christianwriter33@yahoo.com